Contents

Chapter 1

What is climate change?

Spring is coming earlier in some parts of the world; the ice sheets are melting; temperatures are rising. Our planet is getting warmer. What does all this mean, and does it matter? Most scientists believe that human activity is changing the climate on Earth and that this change may have serious and even catastrophic effects. They believe that everyone must think about the way they live to try to halt climate change before the damage becomes irreversible. Some other people think either that there is no significant change, or that human activity is not the cause. It is a complex issue, yet it is one that affects all of us and that we can't afford to ignore.

Is our climate changing?

All scientists who study the climate agree that there have been changes in the world's climate over the last hundred years. In some parts of the world people have kept temperature records for several hundred years. These records show that on average the temperature has risen 0.7° C in the last century. This may not sound like much, but it is enough to make some very real differences, including:

- **melting ice**. The North and South poles and the areas around them – the Arctic and Antarctica – have vast ice sheets that stretch for hundreds of kilometres. Yet over the last few years, these ice sheets have reduced in size as rising temperatures have caused them to melt. Glaciers (frozen rivers) in mountainous areas all over Earth are also melting.

- **melting permafrost**. Permafrost is a layer of permanently frozen ground that is found in very cold regions. Such ground may not always be covered with snow or ice, but it

Expert View

Scientists believe it is 90 per cent certain that humans have affected the climate:

'It is *extremely likely* that human activities have exerted a substantial net warming influence on climate since 1750.'

Intergovernmental Panel on Climate Change, 2007

Is Our Climate Changing?

Anne Rooney

W

FRA ATTS

First published in 2008 by Franklin Watts

Franklin Watts
338 Euston Road
London NW1 3BH

Franklin Watts Australia
Level 17/207 Kent Street, Sydney, NSW 2000

Produced by Arcturus Publishing Limited,
26/27 Bickels Yard, 151–153 Bermondsey Street, London SE1 3HA

Series concept: Alex Woolf
Editor: Nicola Barber
Designer: Ian Winton
Illustrations: Stefan Chabluk

Picture credits:
The Bridgeman Art Library: 12 (Private Collection).
Corbis: cover and 7 (Paul Souders), 9 (NASA/ Roger Ressmeyer), 10 (Tomas Bravo/ epa), 11 (Martin Ruetschi/ Keystone), 13 (Francis Latreille), 17 (Ryan Pyle), 20 (Liu Liqun), 23 (Andrea Merola/ epa), 25 (CDC/ PHIL), 26 (Bettmann), 31 (Michael Macor/ San Francisco Chronicle), 33 (Saipul Siagiancheers/ handout/ epa), 35 (Fritz Hoffmann), 36 (Ashley Cooper), 41 (Gideon Mendel), 43 (Jacques Langevin/ Corbis Sygma).
NASA: 40 (Christopher Shuman, ICESat Deputy Project Scientist, Goddard Space Flight Center. Artists' rendering Greg Shirah and Alex Kekesi, Scientific Visualizations Studio, Goddard Space Flight Center).
Science Photo Library: 8, 18 (Gary Hincks), 14 (British Antarctic Survey), 29 (Tony Craddock), 30 (US Department of Energy), 37 (Sinclair Stammers).
Shutterstock: title page and 27 (Jan Martin Will), 38 (Markus Gann).

Every attempt has been made to clear copyright. Should there be any inadvertent omission, please apply to the publisher for rectification.

A CIP catalogue record for this book is available from the British Library.

Dewey Decimal Classification Number: 363.738'74

ISBN 978 0 7496 8217 0

Printed in China

Franklin Watts is a division of Hachette Children's Books, an Hachette Livre UK company.
www.hachettelivre.co.uk

never normally melts completely because the average temperatures in these regions are so low. In recent times permafrost has been melting in some areas for the first time in centuries.

• *earlier seasons*. The arrival of spring is indicated by natural events such as birds nesting and flowers blooming. In many places these events are happening earlier than usual because the temperatures that trigger them occur earlier in the year. In Europe, plants are flowering on average 2.5 days earlier than ten years ago; around the world, the average is 5.1 days earlier.

• *moving plants and animals*. Plants and animals are being found in new areas as the climate changes. Some places are becoming too hot, too dry or too wet to sustain particular animals or plants. Other regions have become warmer, offering the ideal climate for new species.

Water pours from a melting iceberg in Disko Bay, Greenland.

The years 1998 and 2000 to 2005 were the hottest on record. Temperatures have been recorded in Britain since 1659. Over this whole period, twenty of the twenty-one hottest years have occurred since 1980, and 2005 saw the highest average temperatures of all.

Why the climate changes

Climate scientists believe that the changes we are seeing now are the result of greenhouse gases building up in the atmosphere. Greenhouse gases are a group of gases that collect in a layer at the top of the atmosphere and act rather like an insulating blanket, keeping heat close to Earth. They are called 'greenhouse gases' because they behave rather like the glass walls and roof of a greenhouse – they trap heat to keep Earth warm. Carbon dioxide, methane and water vapour are all examples of greenhouse gases.

Hotter and hotter

The Earth is heated by the sun. About one-third of the heat energy from the sun is reflected straight back into space by clouds and dust in the atmosphere; about one-fifth warms up the atmosphere around Earth and about half actually reaches the surface of Earth. Some of the heat energy that reaches Earth is reflected back – particularly from the polar ice caps – and up into the atmosphere again. Some of this reflected heat passes back through the atmosphere and into space, but some is trapped by clouds and greenhouse gases. The layer of greenhouse gases reduces the amount of reflected heat that can pass from the Earth to space. Instead, the heat is reflected back from the blanket of gases to the surface once more, warming Earth again.

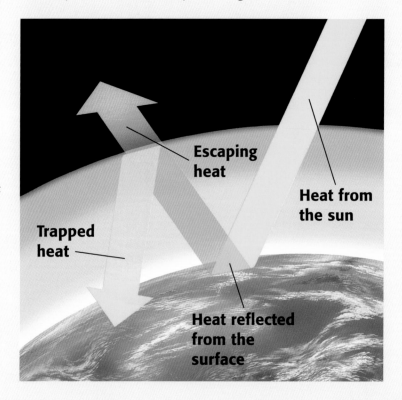

Escaping heat

Heat from the sun

Trapped heat

Heat reflected from the surface

Although some of the heat from the sun is reflected back into space, some is trapped by the layer of greenhouse gases and remains to warm the surface of the Earth.

Too much atmosphere – and too little

The Earth's atmosphere has supported life for millions of years. Near neighbours of Earth in the solar system show what it's like to have too little atmosphere, or too thick a layer of greenhouse gases. They are not planets on which humans could live. Venus is Earth's nearest neighbour in space. It has a dense atmosphere that is 94 per cent carbon dioxide, producing an extreme greenhouse effect. This atmosphere traps heat near the planet's surface, producing scalding temperatures of around 467° C.

The surface of Venus is extremely hot. Heat from the sun is trapped by a thick layer of the greenhouse gas carbon dioxide.

Expert View

Although some politicians and business figures like to suggest that the existence of climate change is still being debated, there is no disagreement amongst scientists about the reality of climate change:

'Consensus as strong as the one that has developed around this topic [climate change] is rare in science.'

Donald Kennedy, Editor-in-Chief, Science, *2001*

Mercury is the planet closest to the sun. It has virtually no atmosphere and as a result the temperature on the planet's surface fluctuates wildly. The average temperature on the side of Mercury that is facing the sun is 427° C; on the side that is facing away it is −173° C. Because Mercury spins very slowly on its axis, each 'day' on Mercury is longer than the planet's year of 88 Earth-days.

Effects of climate change

You might not think that you would notice a difference of only 0.7° C in the temperature – and if the only effect were to make the air a little warmer, you would probably be right. But a rise in temperature – even a small one – has quite significant effects on the world around us.

Weather systems are very sensitive to even the slightest changes. A small rise (or drop) in temperature can be enough to trigger a tropical storm instead of a wind, a drought instead of a dry spell, or a flood instead of a rainy period. Extreme weather events such as heat waves and tropical storms are becoming more frequent. These events can have serious direct impacts – people often die in heat waves, floods and tropical storms – but they also have other, more indirect, effects. They change conditions for farming, for example, sometimes causing crop failures that can lead to famines. Even weather that appears less severe can create problems. A winter that is milder than normal with fewer frosts and less snow means that more pests can survive to damage crops or cause disease in the following year.

Drought causes crops to fail. In this field of corn (maize), between 70 and 90 per cent of the crop was lost because there was not enough rain.

FORUM

People hold different views about the human contribution to climate change:

'[The] human contribution is not significant and … observed increases in carbon dioxide and other greenhouse gases make only a negligible contribution to climate warming.'

Professor David H. Douglass, University of Rochester (International Journal of Climatology, 2007)

'Humans are changing the Earth, and it's a big effect we're having.'

Mike MacCracken, chief scientist for climate change projects at the Climate Institute in Washington D.C.

What do you think?

Extreme weather can eventually make some areas uninhabitable. In some places desertification is already a problem. As populations increase people put more demands on the land, clearing it to grow crops and taking more water from wells. These actions, often combined with less than average rainfall, result in the land drying out. As the land turns into desert, the types of plants that can survive also change: grassland and crops are replaced by tough scrub that needs little water. These plants cannot support people or livestock, and make the land unusable by humans.

How we use the weather

In many parts of the world people have built their livelihoods on known and reliable weather patterns. Crops and livestock are particularly weather-dependent: as the climate changes people may have to think again about the crops they grow and the foods they eat. Areas that depend on tourism may also find that their income is affected as the weather changes. Some low-lying ski resorts may have less snow, and some seaside resorts may become too hot and dry, or too prone to storms, to attract customers.

In some ski resorts, snowfall has decreased to such an extent that artificial snow is used to cover the pistes.

Chapter 2

Has the climate changed in the past?

Climate change is not new. The climate has changed throughout history and prehistory, sometimes in very extreme ways.

Hot and cold

There is plenty of evidence for climate change in the past. Some historical documents are good sources of information about the climate of a particular period, even if they do not record actual temperatures. For example, we know from written accounts that there was a period during the Middle Ages when temperatures were warmer than they had been in previous centuries, at least in the area around the North Atlantic Ocean. Between the ninth and thirteenth centuries people could grow grapes for wine-making in quite northerly areas of Europe. The ice-free northern seas also allowed the Vikings to explore Iceland from 874 and Greenland from 985.

This contemporary engraving of a frost fair on the River Thames, England, in the winter of 1683 to 1684, shows that winters were colder in the seventeenth century than they are today.

This trend reversed during the sixteenth to nineteenth centuries, when Europe experienced a 'little ice age'. Around 1250 Arctic pack ice started to expand and the reliable warm summers of the Middle Ages ended. By the mid-seventeeth century some glaciers in the Alps had extended far enough to crush villages in their paths.

Winters became colder, causing rivers and canals in Northern Europe and North America to freeze over. Since the mid-nineteenth century, the climate has been warming again. Few scientists dispute that warming *is* happening, but there is no universal agreement about *why* it is happening.

Prehistoric climate change

We know that in the distant past there have been several true ice ages, when temperatures over the whole of our planet fell far lower than they are today. The last ice age ended around 10,000 years ago, at a time when human beings were well established on Earth but had not yet begun to build civilizations.

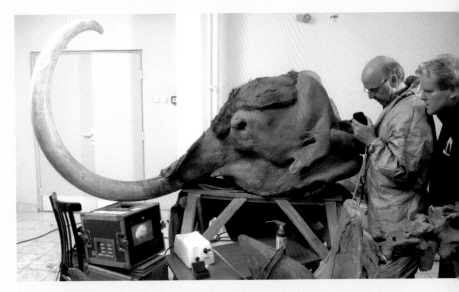

The well-preserved remains of this mammoth were recovered from the permafrost in Siberia. Mammoths lived during the last ice age.

Some scientists believe that mass extinction events may be caused by climate change. Mass extinctions occur on average every 26 million years and wipe out many of the species living on Earth. A mass extinction event ended the era of the dinosaurs, 65 million years ago. It is likely that this event was caused by climate change, possibly triggered by an asteroid hitting Earth or a series of massive volcanic eruptions. Either of these cataclysmic natural disasters could have caused climate change on a vast scale, either because dust in the air blocked heat energy from the sun and made the Earth colder, or because a thick blanket of greenhouse gases trapped heat and made the Earth warmer.

FOCUS

Salty water

David and Mary Mallia have an organic fruit farm in Malta, an island in the Mediterranean. Like other people on Malta, they draw fresh water from a bore hole which is usually replenished by rain. In recent years, there has been less rain and the sea level has risen. The water in the bore hole is now becoming salty and can no longer be used for irrigating the Mallias' crops. "If you water your trees with this water, it will kill them," David says.

How we know

The natural world around us is full of clues about the climate changes that occurred before human history began. Scientific evidence for climate change can be gleaned from the fossil record, from ice cores, from tree rings and from box cores drilled from the ocean bed.

The fossil record gives us an indication of where plants and animals lived in the past. For example, fossils of woolly mammoths found near London show that this region was once as cold as Siberia is today.

Scientists drill long tubes of ice, called ice cores, from the ice sheets in the Arctic and Antarctica to find out about the atmosphere in the distant past. They take their data from bubbles of air that are preserved in the ice. They have found that there is more carbon dioxide in the atmosphere today than there has been at any time in the last 800,000 years. At the start of the Industrial Revolution (see page 16), in the late eighteenth century, carbon dioxide made up 0.028 per cent of Earth's atmosphere. By 2005, this level was 0.038 per cent. Before the twentieth century the fastest rise in the level of carbon dioxide was 0.00003 per cent over 1,000 years, but the level rose by this amount over only 17 years between 1989 and 2006.

Scientists remove an ice core taken from Antarctica. The air bubbles trapped in the ice provide valuable information about the atmosphere in the past.

The study of the past through the examination of tree rings, both in living trees and those that have been preserved or fossilized, is called dendrochronology. The thickness of the growth rings of a tree tells scientists about the conditions in which the tree grew, including the temperature and concentration of gases in the atmosphere. Box cores are plugs of sediment that have been removed from the sea floor. They can provide evidence of cataclysmic events such as floods and landslides, which are often related to climate.

It's not just us

The fact that the climate changed in the prehistoric past proves that climate change is not always related to human behaviour. The climate can be altered by activity on the sun itself, which leads to hotter or colder weather on Earth. It is also affected by natural events on Earth such as volcanic eruptions or large wildfires.

When a volcano erupts it hurls gas and dust high into the atmosphere. These volcanic gases include carbon dioxide and water vapour, both of which are greenhouse gases. Volcanic dust can block heat and light from the sun for several years after an eruption, causing a temporary cooling effect. A massive eruption of the Indonesian volcano Tambora in 1815 produced colder weather around the world that year and the next. Temperatures dropped by up to 3° C and 1815 was known as 'the year without a summer'. A volcanic eruption can also kill plants, so they are not able to remove the excess carbon dioxide from the air. The smoke and ash from wildfires have a similar effect on the atmosphere.

FORUM

People hold different views about whether the changes in the climate that are noticeable now have been brought about by human action:

'Climate change is a natural phenomenon. Climate keeps changing all the time. The fact that climate changes is not in itself a threat, because, obviously, in the past human beings have adapted to all kinds of climate changes.'

S. Fred Singer, atmospheric physicist at George Mason University, USA

'All published scientific investigations of the causes of 20th century warming have consistently found that natural factors alone cannot explain the warming.'

Michael Mann, Stefan Rahmstorf, Gavin Schmidt, Eric Steig and William Connolley, www.realclimate.org

What's your view?

Chapter 3

Are we changing the climate?

Scientists know that the climate alters slowly – there is enough evidence from the past to show that it can change regardless of human activity. Most scientists also agree that the rise in global temperatures that has occurred over the last century, and which is speeding up, *is* caused by human actions.

How do we change the climate?

The modern industrial age started in the West in the late eighteenth century with the Industrial Revolution. At that time, people began to invent machinery that was powered by coal, gas and oil. The rapid development of technology in the nineteenth and twentieth centuries has changed the way people live. All around the planet, millions of people burn fuels such as coal, gas and oil to produce electricity, to power vehicles and other machinery, and to keep their homes warm. Coal, gas and oil are all fossil fuels.

Fossil fuels were formed over millions of years from the bodies of once-living organisms, both plants and animals. The carbon contained in the organisms remains in the fossil fuel until it is burned. When it is burned, the carbon combines with oxygen in the air to form carbon dioxide. This carbon dioxide escapes into the atmosphere and adds to the blanket of greenhouse gases that surrounds our planet.

FOCUS

Warmer seas

Mikami Hideshige is the leader of the fishermen's association in Kafuka, on the Japanese island of Rebun. The community relies on fishing for herring and cod, but because the sea has got warmer the fish are staying away – they need cold seas in which to breed. The fishermen's catch reduced by between 20 and 30 per cent in 2005-6. "We live on what we earn in the summertime as we lose money fishing in the winter. But now we don't have anything left to save," he says.

'Slash and burn' land clearance involves cutting down and burning forested areas to free land for agriculture. Sixty years ago, this region of southern China was covered with tropical rainforest. Today there is little of the rainforest left.

The production of carbon dioxide from fossil fuels is not the only way in which human activity is changing the climate. Some farming practices contribute to the problem. In many places people cut down trees or burn forests to clear land for growing crops. In doing so they destroy trees that help to remove carbon dioxide from the atmosphere (see page 18). The burning of trees also produces carbon dioxide. Livestock farming adds to the level of greenhouse gases because the animals breathe out carbon dioxide. Livestock are also major producers of another greenhouse gas, methane (see page 19).

Fossil fuels and the carbon cycle

The bodies of all living things are made of organic compounds – chemicals that include carbon in their structure. Animals obtain this carbon from the food they eat, whether it is plants or other animals. All animals breathe in oxygen and breathe out carbon dioxide. Plants obtain carbon from the atmosphere. During the process of photosynthesis, green plants take carbon dioxide in, remove the carbon for use in building their own structures, and release oxygen into the atmosphere.

When a plant or animal dies, it may be eaten, it may decay, or its body may very slowly change into a fossil fuel. If the body is eaten, the carbon passes to the animal that eats it and is locked up in the predator's body until it dies. If the body decays, the carbon is released into the atmosphere, soil or water. If it turns into a fossil fuel, the carbon stays locked away for millions of years. Over the last two hundred years people have begun to burn large quantities of fossil fuels, releasing all the previously locked-away carbon into the atmosphere. At the same time, people have cut down large areas of trees that could help to take the extra carbon dioxide out of the air and convert it into oxygen.

The carbon cycle shows how carbon dioxide moves into and out of the atmosphere through living things and the Earth.

Carbon dioxide cycle

Photosynthesis

Plant respiration

Animal respiration

Marine life respiration

Car and factory emissions

Volcanic activity

Decaying plant material

Marine plant photosynthesis

Dead organisms and waste products

Marine organisms

Underseas volcanoes

Dissolved gases in magma

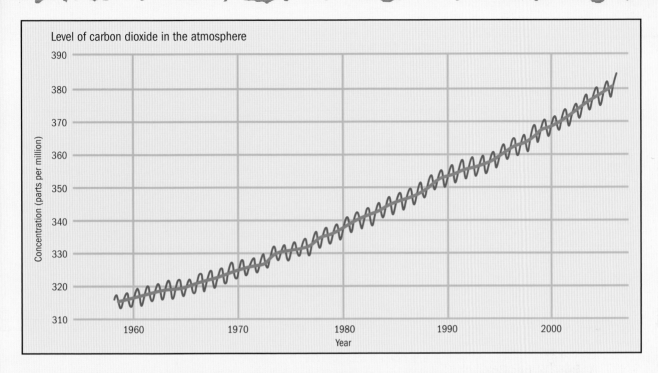

In 1957 the American scientist Roger Revelle suggested that population growth and industrial activity would lead to increased levels of carbon dioxide in the air, and that this would have disastrous effects. Scientists have measured levels of atmospheric carbon dioxide ever since. The graph above shows that the amount is steadily rising. The blue zigzags are caused by seasonal (summer/winter) variations in carbon dioxide levels.

Methane: cookers and cows

Methane is a natural gas, made of carbon and hydrogen. People extract methane gas from under the ground and under the sea to burn as a fuel. When methane is burned, carbon from the gas combines with oxygen in the air to make carbon dioxide, while the hydrogen combines with oxygen to make water. Methane is also produced in some industrial processes and as a by-product of livestock farming. The digestive processes of cattle create high levels of methane, which is then released directly into the atmosphere. Methane gas is even more effective as a greenhouse gas than carbon dioxide.

Expert View

'[There] is an unequivocal series of evidence [showing that] fossil fuel burning and land use change are affecting the climate on our planet.'

'If you are an African child born in 2007, by the time you are 50 years old you may be faced with disease and new levels of drought.'

Achim Steiner, Executive Director of the United Nations Environment Programme, 2007

Predicting the future

The most recent computer models predict that the average temperature on Earth will probably rise between 1.8° C and 4° C by 2100, but the increase could be as much as 6.4° C. This difference is as great as that between today and the end of the last ice age 10,000 years ago.

Where carbon gases come from

Carbon dioxide is released when people burn fossil fuels, but there are less obvious ways in which we produce carbon gases (carbon dioxide and methane). For example, large amounts of energy and fuel are used to manufacture and transport many items that we take for granted – from ballpoint pens to flat-screen televisions. When we buy food that has been grown abroad, fuel has been burned to move it, often by air. Even farming animals for meat creates considerably more carbon gases than growing vegetables and cereals. All of these are examples of hidden sources of carbon gases. In fact, almost every aspect of life in the industrialized world contributes to climate change.

Who is producing carbon?

The highest levels of carbon gases are produced by developed industrial nations such as those in Europe, North America, Australasia and parts of Southeast Asia because these countries use the most fossil fuels. Countries where industry is developing rapidly are also producing increasing amounts of carbon emissions, particularly China and India.

Power plants such as this one in Hebei Province, China, produce a huge volume of greenhouse gases.

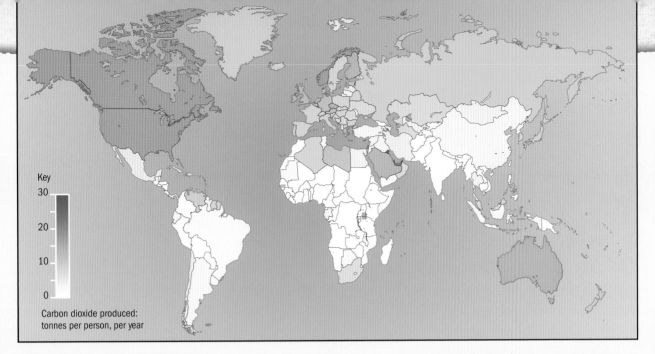

Key
30

20

10

0

Carbon dioxide produced:
tonnes per person, per year

The figures used to create this map divide the total annual carbon dioxide production of a country by its population. Some people produce much more carbon dioxide than others. People who use a lot of fossil fuels have a large carbon footprint. People who use less have a smaller carbon footprint.

FORUM

Should the countries that are responsible for climate change be responsible for sorting it out, or must all nations act together?

'If the poor, developing countries are not responsible for climate change, then why should they have to pay the price for what the industrialized countries have done?'

Jafrul Islam Chowdhury, Bangladeshi State Minister for the Environment

'The consequences of global climate change are so pressing, it doesn't matter who was responsible for the past. What matters is who is answerable for the future. And that is all of us.'

Arnold Schwarzenegger, Governor of California

What do you think about this?

Until 2006, the United States produced more carbon dioxide than any other country in the world, but China is now the largest producer. This is not because the United States is producing less of the gas, but because China is producing more. A more accurate measure is to compare the amount of carbon dioxide against the population of a country. The population of China is far bigger than that of the United States. So, in 2006, every person in the United States was responsible for producing four times as much carbon dioxide as one person in China, and more than 1,500 times as much as one person in the undeveloped African nation of Chad. The carbon dioxide produced by each individual is called a carbon footprint. It is a measure of a person's impact on the planet.

Chapter 4

How will climate change affect us?

Climate change will affect the whole world, altering the environment for people everywhere. It is not just a matter of changing weather: there will be social, political, economic, medical and ecological effects, too.

A warmer, wetter world

As the planet warms up, the ice sheets in the Arctic and Antarctica are melting, pouring more water into the sea. In the Arctic the areas of sea that are covered by ice are getting smaller and the ice is getting thinner. Antarctica is not as badly affected yet, as its ice sheet is much thicker than the Arctic ice, and it sits on top of solid ground. Even so, Antarctica is warming five times faster than other regions of the world. There are several reasons for this. One is that the atmosphere is thinner at the poles so more of the sun's heat reaches the surface. The extra heat melts the ice. In fact, as more and more ice melts, the whole world is likely to warm increasingly quickly. This is because ice sheets reflect 90 per cent of the sun's heat, sending some of it back into space. Sea water, however, is dark and absorbs more of the sun's heat, warming the oceans even further. So, as the ice shrinks and the oceans expand, less heat will be reflected and more absorbed.

Melting ice sheets are not only a problem for the people and animals that live in very cold regions. They could have a huge impact on people in all parts of our planet. The melted water from the ice flows into the seas and oceans and raises sea levels around the world. Thirteen of the twenty largest cities in the

FOCUS

Melting sea ice
The Inuit people live in the very cold regions of the Arctic. As the sea warms and the ice melts, it is becoming increasingly dangerous for the Inuit to set out across the ice to hunt seals. Aqqaluk Lynge says, "When I was a boy in northern Greenland, the sea ice formed in November. Now we don't see it for months after that."

world are on the coast, and more than a third of the world's population lives within 90 kilometres of the sea (one-fifth lives within 30 kilometres of the sea). If the sea level rises just a few metres, large parts of cities such as New York (USA), London (UK), Shanghai (China), and Mumbai (India) will flood. A rise of 10 metres would make 25 per cent of the population of the United States homeless. The sea level has risen 15 centimetres in the last 100 years – that's ten times faster than the average rise over the last 2,000 years.

These boys are using a canoe to move around the flooded square of St Mark's in Venice, Italy. Venice is a low-lying city that often floods. As sea levels rise, floods are becoming increasingly frequent.

Not just the polar ice

Glaciers are vast frozen rivers of ice that flow very slowly down mountains. Since the 1970s, glaciers around the world have been thinning, flowing more quickly and even disappearing completely. Glaciers provide drinking water for one-sixth of the population of the world, and around 75 per cent of the water used to irrigate crops in Central Asia comes from glaciers. Losing the glaciers will have a very serious impact on farming.

Polar regions have a layer of permafrost – ground that is usually permanently frozen (see page 6). As temperatures rise this ground is melting. In places such as Siberia and Alaska some buildings that have been constructed on the frozen ground have collapsed as the ground has softened beneath them. If the ground melts completely it will expose deposits of methane hydrate, which exist under the permafrost. Large amounts of methane would then escape into the atmosphere from these deposits. As methane is a powerful greenhouse gas, global warming may speed up even further.

Changing seasons

As the world warms up, the pattern of seasons is changing. Many people have noticed that spring is arriving earlier in some areas, and that winters are milder. The areas that have tropical and sub-tropical climates are widening, too. These changes mean that animals and plants may be able to – or have to – live in different areas. There could be some benefits: some farmers in the north are already growing crops that need warmer weather conditions. For example, for the first time in history farmers in Greenland can grow potatoes. But there will be serious harmful effects, too. If world temperatures continue to rise, crops that need cool or wet conditions will no longer grow in some places that depend on them. Some regions will become too hot and dry for any kind of agriculture.

Many traditional diets will have to change as the animals and plants on which people once depended will no longer be available. Some traditional practices will also

> ## FOCUS
>
> **Disappearing glaciers**
> Elena Quispe is a 37-year-old Aymara Indian who lives in Bolivia. The fresh water on which her family relies all comes from a glacier in the Andes. By the middle of the twenty-first century, the glaciers that provide Elena's drinking water will be completely gone. "Where are we going to get water?" she asks. "Without water, how can we live?"

disappear. For example, the Inuit bury seal meat in pits in the ground to freeze and preserve it, but this will not be possible if the ground is too warm. By 2025, two-thirds of the world's population could be short of water as a result of lower rainfall and disappearing glaciers. This will lead to terrible hardship and upheaval as people move in search of places to live where they can still grow crops.

Many diseases and parasites also depend on particular temperatures or levels of humidity. The areas affected by deadly tropical diseases such as malaria are growing wider. Malaria has appeared in northern Italy, and will move north through Europe as the mosquitoes that carry it are able to survive in the increasingly warmer conditions.

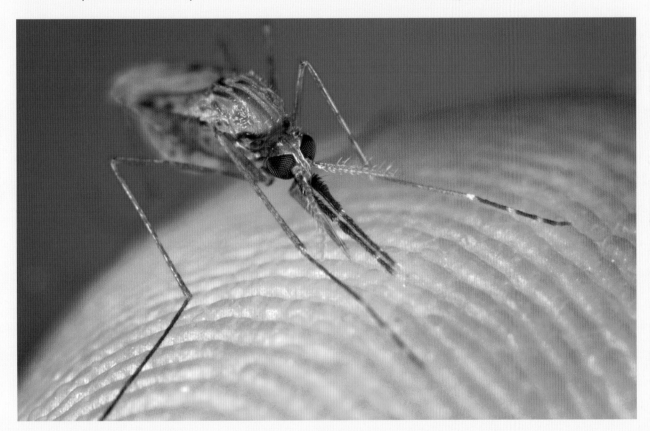

The bite of the female *Anopheles* mosquito is responsible for transmitting malaria between people.

Extreme weather

Warmer air and seas will lead to more extreme weather patterns. Events such as tropical storms and floods, droughts and heat waves, will all be more frequent. Such extreme weather can be devastating in the short term, but it can also have far-reaching long-term effects. Floods and storms can destroy people's homes; drought can wreck livelihoods and change farming patterns.

Heat waves can be very dangerous, particularly for elderly people and young children. In 2003, around 35,000 people died in a heat wave in Europe. Extended periods of hot, dry weather make it easier for wildfires to start and to spread. Wind erosion is another hazard, as the topsoil, the layer of fertile soil in which plants take root, is easily blown away when the ground is completely dried out.

In the 1930s, poor farming practices led to 'dust bowl' conditions in parts of the United States. Vast tracts of farmland were abandoned after the land dried out and the topsoil blew away.

Expert View

'We now have a clearer indication of the potential impact of global warming, some of which is already inevitable ... The challenge is now to support those people living in the most vulnerable areas so that they are able to adapt and improve their ways of life.'

Sir Martin Rees, President of the Royal Society, UK, 2007

The politics of climate change

Some parts of the Earth will become uninhabitable as they become hotter and drier – or wetter. What will happen to the people who live there? In many cases, they will have no choice but to move somewhere else. By 2050 it is likely that 200 million people will have become ecological refugees, forced to move from their homes because they can no longer grow crops, or because they do not have access to water. Such massive migrations are likely to spark wars and social unrest.

Land and sea

Rising sea temperatures will affect the animals and plants that live in the oceans, and the micro-organisms that form the basis of the food chains in the oceans. The sea is full of very small plants called algae. Warmer seas can lead to more algae growing. Algae photosynthesize like plants on the land (see page 18), so they take in carbon dioxide and produce oxygen during the day, but at night they do not produce oxygen and the oxygen level in the sea falls. Algae also lie in an opaque layer on the surface of the ocean, which stops sunlight penetrating the water. Lack of light harms other ocean life beneath the surface, and if the organisms on which fish rely for food cannot survive, the fish will die, too. These are complex issues and scientists disagree about whether an increase in algae would be good or bad for the environment.

People disagree about whether the impact of climate change will be good or bad:

'It's not that there won't be bad things happening in [some] countries. There will be – things like you'll lose polar bears. But the idea is that they will get such large gains, especially in agriculture, that they will be bigger than the losses.'

Robert O. Mendelsohn, Yale School of Forestry & Environmental Studies

'[Significant climate change would] threaten fundamental food and water sources. It would lead to displacement of billions of people and huge waves of refugees, spawn terrorism and topple governments, spread disease across the globe.'

David Appell, science writer

What's your opinion?

Companions on the planet

Climate change is affecting all living things, including plants and animals. Already, polar wildlife is suffering as the ice melts. In the Arctic, polar bears are endangered by the loss of the ice sheets on which they live and hunt. In the southern oceans, penguins are losing their nesting grounds.

Changing seasonal patterns affect plants, and the birds and animals that depend on the plants suffer as a result. Scientists estimate that up to 40 per cent of species may become extinct if the global average temperature rises 2° C above its level in 1990 (around 14.4° C).

Polar bears hunt on the ice sheets and will drown or starve if too much of the ice melts.

Chapter 5

What are we doing about it?

There are two approaches to reducing greenhouse gas emissions. One is to use less energy and burn less fuel. The other is to find alternative sources of energy that produce fewer or no greenhouse gases. Both paths can be pursued together, but each requires action by governments, businesses and individuals. People will need to change their lifestyles – and not all are willing to do so. People disagree, too, about what should or can be done. Tackling climate change is a difficult challenge that faces the whole planet.

Science to the rescue?

The process of developing new sources of energy that do not produce greenhouse gases is a slow one. There are already many alternative energy sources, including solar power, wind power and nuclear power, but they are not widely used. Building power stations to use some of these technologies will take many years. In the meantime, everyone needs to reduce their use of energy to cut carbon dioxide emissions, and science has a role to play in making machinery, vehicles and buildings more energy efficient.

Solar power

Solar power is energy from the sun. The sun pours energy in the form of heat and light on to the Earth. In fact, the sun could easily satisfy all our energy needs forever if we could harness its energy efficiently. Solar panels and solar towers collect energy from the sun. This can be stored, just as electricity is stored in a battery, and used when it is needed. Today's solar panels do not convert all the energy that falls onto them into

Expert View

'As the technology for solar cells gets better and better, this form of clean, renewable energy will find more applications that take up less space and produce more electricity, to meet the energy needs of our homes, schools and businesses.'

Samuel W. Bodman, U.S. Secretary of Energy, 2005

The mirrors of this solar power station in France concentrate energy from the sun onto a focal point in the central tower, heating it to 3,000° C. The energy is used to generate electricity.

usable electricity, but scientists are developing more efficient models. A new and more efficient material for collecting solar energy is a thin, flexible sheet which could be draped over objects. Solar panels have the disadvantage, too, that they only work when the sun shines! They can't generate electricity at night, and they are less efficient on cloudy days and in the winter. The most effective solar power stations are in very sunny places, such as the Middle East, Australia and parts of the United States.

Wind power

Wind power is energy from the wind. The power of the wind has been harnessed for centuries to drive windmills to grind corn and wheat. Modern wind turbines work in the same way as windmills, except that they use the energy from the turning blades to generate electricity instead of turning a millstone.

Wind farms are fields full of wind turbines. The turbines are set up in exposed areas where the wind blows strongly and reliably. Some people object to wind turbines, saying they are ugly and noisy. One solution is to build offshore wind farms, on sandbanks out at sea. The wind at sea is not stopped by features of the landscape or buildings, and the wind turbines are usually sufficiently far away from coasts to avoid annoying people.

Expert View

'Each one of us is a cause of global warming, but each one of us can become part of the solution: in the decisions we make on what we buy, the amount of electricity we use, the cars we drive, and how we live our lives.'

Al Gore, 2006

Nuclear power

Nuclear power is produced by breaking atoms apart. It is possible by this method to produce a lot of energy from a very small amount of fuel. However, nuclear power is not a popular option with the public in many parts of the world because of concerns about accidents and nuclear waste. An accident at the Chernobyl nuclear power plant in the former USSR in 1986 killed many people and caused permanent ill health in thousands of others over a wide area. In all, around 6.6 million people were exposed to dangerous levels of radiation as a result of the accident.

A worker in a nuclear power station stays safely behind a thick glass barrier as he operates machinery to move radioactive waste into sealed containers. The safe disposal of dangerous radioactive waste is a serious problem for the future.

Nuclear power also produces radioactive waste which remains dangerous for thousands of years. Disposing of this waste safely is a problem. In the 1950s and 1960s it was dumped in the sea; today most is in temporary storage while governments and scientists try to agree on safe strategies for its long-term management. The most likely outcome is that this waste will be buried deep under the ground. Many people also worry that if the material needed by and produced by nuclear power stations fell into the hands of terrorists it could be used to make nuclear weapons or 'dirty bombs'.

Powering vehicles

Vehicles such as cars, trucks, ships and planes are a major source of carbon dioxide emissions. Twenty-eight per cent of all the energy used in the United States goes to powering vehicles. While manufacturers try to make vehicles more efficient, scientists search for long-term solutions. Alternative sources of fuel for vehicles include hydrogen cells, electricity, and fuels made from plants (or even algae) called biofuels. Although biofuels produce carbon dioxide when burned, the plants absorb carbon dioxide as they grow. However biofuels are not quite carbon neutral – more carbon dioxide is produced in making and burning them than is absorbed by the growing plants.

This dried corn, being harvested in California, will be used to produce the biofuel ethanol.

Some car manufacturers now make cars that will run on electricity. Such electricity could eventually come from 'green' sources such as solar power, but even electricity obtained from conventional sources is more efficient than burning oil products to run cars. At the moment, electric cars have a short range – a battery can hold enough charge to drive an electric car only about 80 kilometres – and this makes these cars unsuitable for many people. Hybrid cars use both electricity and liquid fuel. They use energy from the car's braking action to recharge the battery, then use the liquid fuel when the battery is exhausted.

Ethanol from plants is already used to run some vehicles. However, the use of ethanol as a fuel has its drawbacks. The plants from which the fuel is obtained are often grown on land that was used for food crops. As a result, less food is grown, causing food prices to rise. Some of the poorest people in Central and South America are already blaming biofuels for the rise in the price of tortilla flour.

International studies

Most people agree that action against climate change must be based on scientific knowledge. There are many scientific programmes around the world that study different aspects of climate change. The most important international work is by the Intergovernmental Panel on Climate Change (IPCC). This is a scientific body that assesses all work on climate change and presents it for governments to use. It produces major reports every five years or so. In its 2007 report the IPCC said that it is 90 per cent likely that the climate change we are seeing now is caused by human activity.

International agreements

Many people – scientists, politicians and others – agree that to reduce the impact of climate change we must reduce

FOCUS

Storm danger

The people of Shishmaref, Alaska, have applied to the US government for money to move their settlement. Their island is being torn apart by storms. Previously, steep ice cliffs protected the island from the worst of the weather, but now the ice is thinning and the storms are worse. It will be 2009 before the residents can move, and they don't know yet where they will go.

"It's not our fault that the permafrost is melting, or that there's global warming," says Luci Eningowuk, who lives in Shishmaref. "Our lives are at stake during the storms."

greenhouse gas emissions. An important international agreement, the Kyoto Protocol, sets out targets for reducing greenhouse gases. It was drawn up in 1997, and most of the major countries in the world have now agreed to it. Only Australia and the United States have not formally accepted its demands. The Kyoto Protocol came into force in 2005. In December 2007, the United States agreed for the first time to engage in negotiation with the rest of the world to reduce emissions. New plans setting targets for all nations will be agreed before 2010.

Activists dressed up as penguins campaign for action on climate change. Penguin colonies are suffering already as a result of warming.

Under the Kyoto Protocol, the European Union aims to reduce greenhouse gas emissions by 8 per cent by the year 2012. The United States is encouraged to reduce emissions by 7 per cent. Canada, Hungary, Japan and Poland aim to reduce emissions by 6 per cent. (Hungary and Poland were not in the EU at the time of the agreement.)

The UK must reduce emissions by 12.5 per cent by 2012. Currently, it is on target to achieve this. Indeed, the UK government predicts that emissions will be cut by 23.6 per cent, which is 11.1 per cent more than its target.

National measures

Those countries that have agreed to the Kyoto Protocol have begun to put measures in place to cut their greenhouse gas emissions. Some of these measures are in the form of new laws, but there are other ways of encouraging people to be more energy efficient, and to discourage the wasteful use of energy. In the UK, for example, people can apply for grants to help pay for insulation in their homes. Insulating a house can make a marked difference to the amount of fuel used to heat it, resulting in lower carbon dioxide emissions. Governments may also encourage the use of alternative sources of energy that don't produce emissions. In Germany, the government provides money to build responsibly and insists on higher standards of energy efficiency than many other nations. New houses are built with high levels of insulation, and solar power plants provide electricity for some communities.

Changing lives

At the moment, there is no quick and easy fix that will put a stop to carbon emissions, and in the near future they are bound to go up, not down. While people in the developed world might be persuaded to settle for the current level of emissions or even reduce them a little, people in the developing world want to be able to enjoy some of the benefits of an industrialized society. Emissions from China, India, Africa and other developing areas will increase as their use of fossil fuels increases. In countries that have democratic

FORUM

People hold different views on the impact individuals can have on climate change:

'Almost half of [the 1,000 British people] interviewed thought changing their behaviour would make no difference to climate change.'

Alex Kirby for the BBC, 2004

'The battle against climate change is not going to be won through anything that happens at the United Nations, nor in Westminster, Washington or Brussels. It is going to be won through countless millions of individual decisions and actions, taken every day, by people who are both concerned enough, and empowered enough, to make a difference. And, if you decide to do so, you can be one of those too.'

HRH Prince Charles, Prince of Wales

Do you think you can make a difference?

Many goods for Western consumption are made in the Far East – like these components for baby buggies being made in China. Is it fair to count the carbon dioxide produced in their manufacture as part of China's emissions?

elections, governments are reluctant to force people to do things. Unpopular measures, such as the imposition of higher taxes, mean that a government is likely to be voted out. Most democratic governments also favour a free market – an economic system in which people can buy what they want, and in which prices are set by how much is available and market demand (supply and demand). Governments are reluctant to interfere with this system. For this reason, obvious solutions such as banning large cars or unnecessary air travel are not adopted. However, surveys suggest that many people are willing to change their lifestyles to fight climate change. In a poll of 22,000 people around the world in 2007, the BBC found that 70 per cent of those questioned were willing to make changes to protect the planet.

Chapter 6

What else can we do?

While better, cleaner fuels are being developed, there are other measures you can take to reduce your carbon footprint and other solutions that science may be able to offer.

Under lock and key

One option is to 'lock up' carbon by burying it underground or at the bottom of the sea so that it can't escape into the atmosphere. This is called sequestration. Carbon dioxide can be removed from waste gases or even from the air by chemical methods and

FOCUS

Disappearing mangroves

Bashunto Janna, 81, used to live on the island of Lochachara, India, where he farmed 85 acres. Now he has one acre on a nearby island where many other people from his community have also moved. Lochachara has completely disappeared, a victim of rising sea levels. It was part of the Sundarbans, an area of mangrove forest between India and Bangladesh. As the mangroves are swallowed by the sea, the people and animals that live here – including the Bengal tiger – are left without homes.

Mangrove forests or mangals, such as this area in Fiji, are found along coastlines in tropical and subtropical regions. These forests are in danger of destruction as sea levels rise.

pumped to the bottom of a deep ocean. On the seabed, it forms a solid compound that dissolves very slowly. Solid waste that will slowly release carbon dioxide as it decays could also be dumped on the deep sea bed directly. An example of waste that could be treated in this way is corn stalks from farming. Such waste would quickly be covered with silt and lie buried for centuries.

Carbon dioxide could be chilled until it turns into liquid, then buried underground by pumping it into emptied oil wells and coal seams. This is already done to a small degree. Another option is to force carbon dioxide to react with rocks to form stable minerals that tie up the carbon.

Eat carbon!

Plants and trees have been removing carbon dioxide from the atmosphere for millions of years. Planting more trees and encouraging plant growth will help with this process. But while there is limited space on land, the oceans offer more scope for using plants to remove carbon dioxide.

Like plants on land, algae need carbon dioxide to grow, but they also need extra nutrients. Long tubes could be used to bring nutrient-rich water from deep down in the sea to feed the algae on the surface. Another possibility is to add nutrients to the surface of the water to encourage the growth of algae. However, it is not

Salps are small transparent creatures that feed on algae. Swarms of them hoover up carbon-rich algae. They expel the carbon as hard pellets that sink to the bottom of the sea.

necessarily safe to alter the sea in this way – it may disrupt the ecology of the seas and oceans in ways we cannot predict, so more research is needed before algae farming is attempted on a large scale.

Carbon trading

Carbon trading, or emissions trading, is a system that allows people or businesses to buy and sell the right to produce greenhouse gases. To start with everyone has the same allowance – this is the amount of carbon dioxide they are permitted to produce. If one person uses up all their allowance they can buy more from someone who doesn't need theirs. If this system were introduced, individuals could choose either to adapt their lifestyles in order to limit their carbon dioxide production to their allowance, or to pay in order to exceed their allowance. Some carbon trading is already being used by large businesses, but the idea could work for individuals, households, businesses or even whole nations.

Changing lifestyles

We will all need to adjust our lifestyles, both to avoid further damage to the climate and to adapt to the changes that are already happening. At the moment, we add a total of 26 billion tonnes of carbon dioxide to the atmosphere each year – more than 4 tonnes for everyone on the planet.

Solar panels on the roof of this house provide free electricity from a renewable source with no carbon emissions.

Already people in many parts of the world are taking more notice of how they contribute to climate change by using energy. Many people are insulating their homes, using energy-efficient light bulbs and equipment, and reducing their use of heating and air-conditioning. Some people are installing solar panels or considering wind power, and looking at hybrid cars. People are beginning to ask whether it is acceptable to drive an unnecessarily large car, or to fly to exotic locations on holiday. As public awareness grows, more people will be willing to give up some aspects of their carbon-hungry lifestyles.

Working together

If humanity is to face the immense challenge of tackling climate change, all nations need to work together. Governments must be prepared to pass laws that may be unpopular, and nations must act responsibly to help one another. Our goal should be for carbon-neutral human existence on the planet. This means that we don't have any harmful impact through our activities.

FORUM

Some people believe governments should take the lead in combating climate change, while others believe businesses or individuals must act first:

'It's easy to feel overwhelmed and powerless – skeptical that individual efforts can really have an impact. But we need to resist that response, because this crisis will get resolved only if we as individuals take responsibility for it.'

Al Gore, winner of Nobel Prize for Peace for work on climate change

'Business is ready to move into the low-emissions era, but needs the appropriate policy framework from government to do so.'

Yvo de Boer, United Nations climate secretariat

Who do you think should lead the way?

Poorer and developing nations are at the moment contributing the least to the problem. But they will need help from richer, developed nations to improve conditions for their people while still protecting the planet. At the same time, rich, developed nations must cut back on their own extravagant use of fossil fuels and unsustainable production of greenhouse gases. We must also put in place a safety net for those who will suffer first, and most severely, as a result of climate change.

Chapter 7

What will happen next?

What will happen now depends on how much we do to tackle climate change. Some consequences of past actions can't now be avoided. Even if we stopped producing more carbon dioxide tomorrow, the average global temperature would still rise by 0.5° C as the carbon dioxide already in the atmosphere makes its effects felt. Of course, carbon dioxide production won't stop tomorrow. So what will happen?

Rising sea levels

In places, the ice in Antarctica is as much as 4 kilometres thick, while in the Arctic the average thickness is about 3 metres. A giant ice shelf in west Antarctica is balanced on the land, but if its base starts to melt it could easily slip into the sea. If either this shelf, or the dome of ice on Greenland in the Arctic, slipped into the sea, the result would be a worldwide rise in sea levels of around 6 metres. This rise would be enough to flood huge areas of heavily populated areas. Countries such as Bangladesh and the Netherlands could be submerged completely. Up to one-third of the world's population could be made homeless. Even if sea levels rise by only 1 metre, the effect will still be disastrous, affecting 6 million people in Egypt, 13 million in Bangladesh, and 72 million in China, as well others around the world.

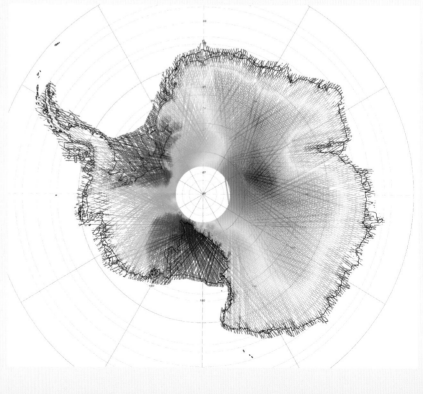

Colour coding shows the height of the Antarctic ice sheet above sea level. Sea level is dark blue; the lowest areas are turquoise and the highest areas are red. The western ice shelf is the low-lying area on the left.

Manjai Sah outside his house in Pir-muhammadpur village, India. The village was flooded twice in 2007, making many people homeless.

Changing weather patterns

We will have to get used to more extreme weather conditions: more heat waves and droughts in some places, but more floods and storms in others. In some parts of the world, it may even get colder. The Gulf Stream is a current of warm water that flows from the Gulf of Mexico through the Atlantic Ocean towards the United Kingdom and northern Europe. It helps to keep temperatures higher than would otherwise be expected in parts of northern Europe. For example, London is nearly as far north as Warsaw in Poland – and further north than Vancouver in Canada – but London enjoys a far warmer climate than either Warsaw or Vancouver. If the Gulf Stream is disrupted by climate change, London and other parts of Europe may become colder.

Expert View

'We're locked into a temperature increase of about 0.5 [C] degrees by 2025 regardless of what we do, but the increases start to diverge depending on the levels of emissions when you look a hundred years from now. So what we do now can make a difference.'

John Fyfe, Canadian Center for Climate Modelling, 2007

Fish stocks will be affected by changing temperatures. Dissolving carbon dioxide will make the sea more acidic, and this will make it difficult for shellfish and corals to form their hard shells. This will affect the food chain, making it harder for fish and sea mammals further up the food chain to survive. Patterns of disease and other health problems will also change as tropical diseases move into new areas and climate-related medical conditions increase.

Political turmoil

Many people will be forced to change the way they live. It is likely that people will move away from areas that have become either too hot and dry, or too wet. This is already happening in the region of Darfur in Sudan. Rainfall in Sudan has fallen by 40 per cent in the last 50 years, causing an extended drought. This drought has led to increasing desertification, which has forced nomads to take their livestock further south than usual into areas occupied by settled farmers, and this is one of the major factors in the long-running war in Darfur. Such struggles over resources will only increase as supplies of water, and land that is suitable for grazing and farming, become increasingly scarce in more areas.

A tipping point

Some scientists think that there is a 'tipping point' – a point at which climate change will have gone too far to be reversed. At that point the world will spiral towards ecological catastrophe. No one can say exactly where the tipping point may be or when it will be reached. This makes it all the more urgent for us to find solutions to the problems and deal with climate change quickly. There are several points where a positive feedback loop will produce escalating problems. For example, as ice melts and flows into the sea, so sea levels rise and reach further up the edges of ice sheets, encouraging further melting. It is impossible to break the cycle once a positive feedback loop such as this starts.

FORUM

Is there any point at all in tackling climate change, or is the problem so large we can't make a difference?

'It is fun to plant trees when you fly, but they make no impact on short-term energy crises and long-term environmental problems.'

David Howell, former energy minister, UK

'Should we fail to rise to this challenge I don't believe we will be able to explain ourselves to future generations that we have let down.'

Tony Blair, former prime minister, UK

What do you think?

These people live in a lake village in Thailand, with floating houses and boats. More people may have to live like this if sea levels continue to rise.

Learning to live in a hotter world

There is much that we can do to make living in a hotter world possible. In areas with more sun, we can increase our use of solar power. Desalination plants can be used to remove salt from sea water and provide clean drinking water in places where there is a shortage of fresh water. Using biotechnology, we can introduce new varieties of crops that will tolerate different conditions. There is already a new variety of rice that will withstand being completely submerged by flood waters. Such measures can be used to help all the world's people to attain a better standard of living, even in the face of climate change.

Glossary

asteroid A rocky or metallic object that orbits the sun but which is too small to be called a planet.

atmosphere The layer of air that surrounds the Earth.

biofuel A fuel made from plant material or biologically-based waste.

biotechnology Technology that is based on biology.

carbon footprint The measure of the amount of carbon gases an individual is responsible for producing.

climate The average weather over time in a particular place.

dendrochronology The study of the past by the examination of the growth rings in trees.

desertification The process by which an area changes into an infertile desert because of lack of rainfall and increased demands from the local population.

dirty bomb A weapon that distributes radioactive material.

drought A period of extreme dryness that results when rainfall drops far below the normal average for a long time.

extinct No longer surviving anywhere on Earth.

famine A lack of food supplies that causes starvation amongst a population.

fossil fuel A fuel made from fossilized biological material – principally oil, gas and coal.

glacier A frozen river that flows very slowly.

greenhouse effect The action of the layer of greenhouse gases in the atmosphere that trap heat close to the Earth and prevent its escape into space.

greenhouse gas A gas that contributes to the greenhouse effect – principally carbon dioxide, methane and water vapour.

heat wave A period of unusually hot weather.

ice age A period when ice covers more of the Earth's surface than usual, and when global temperatures drop.

ice core A long tube of ice drilled from an ice sheet.

ice sheet The thick layer of ice found near the North and South poles which has remained frozen for thousands of years.

insulation The process of preventing the flow of energy (such as heat or electricity).

malaria A tropical, blood-borne disease that causes many deaths worldwide each year. It is carried by mosquitoes.

pack ice Ice that forms from sea water during the winter.

parasite An organism that lives in or on another organism.

permafrost A layer of permanently frozen ground.

photosynthesis The process by which green plants take in carbon dioxide from the atmosphere, and release oxygen into the atmosphere.

positive feedback loop A system in which the results of an action or event prompt the action or event to continue, so reinforcing the result in a continuing cycle.

radiation The emission of energy from matter as a result of the gradual decay of the atoms.

refugee A person who has been displaced from his or her home region, often because of war or a natural disaster.

sediment Matter that is deposited by rivers, glaciers or wind.

sequestration Locking away (carbon) in a form that will prevent it entering the atmosphere for a long time.

silt Fine sand or soil deposited as a sediment by running water.

tipping point The point at which a process has gone so far that it cannot be reversed but will inevitably continue.

tropical storm A violent circular storm with high winds and rainstorms, experienced in tropical and sub-tropical regions.

turbine A rotary engine that takes energy from the flow of a fluid (gas or liquid).

wildfire A fire that runs out of control, usually through forest or scrubland.

Further information

Books

An Inconvenient Truth: Young Adult Version by Al Gore, Bloomsbury, 2007

Weird Weather: Everything You Didn't Want to Know about Climate Change, But Probably Should Find Out by Kate Evans, Groundwood Books, 2007

I Count: Your step-by-step guide to climate bliss by I Count, Penguin, 2006

The Down to Earth Guide to Global Warming by Laurie David and Cambria Gordon, Scholastic, 2007

Films

An Inconvenient Truth, Laurence Bender Productions, 2006
   Full-length movie about climate change and what we can do about it.
www.youtube.com/watch?v=ntOjGVRimPc (user: EUTube)
   How climate change is affecting Europe and how we can adapt to live with it.

Websites

http://news.bbc.co.uk/1/hi/in_depth/629/629/6528979.stm
   A quick guide to how climate change is affecting different parts of the world.

www.icount.org.uk/
   Click on Climate Chaos for a guide to what causes climate change and the impact it will have on people.

www.climatechallenge.gov.uk/understand.html
   Understand climate change and calculate your own carbon footprint.

http://ec.europa.eu/environment/climat/campaign/index_en.htm
   EU guide to what you can do to reduce your carbon emissions.

http://www.foe.co.uk/campaigns/climate/index.html
   Friends of the Earth rundown on climate change.

Index

Entries in **bold** are for pictures.